Little and the Bees

Story by Jenny Giles
Illustrations by Rachel Tonkin

The chimps went for a walk in the forest.

Little Chimp sat on
Mother Chimp's back.

Little Chimp saw some bees.
They came flying out
of a tree.

Big Chimp saw the bees, too.
He looked at the bees,
and he looked at the tree.

Big Chimp walked up
to the tree,
and he hit it.

Some bees came flying out!

Buzz, buzz, buzz,
went the bees.
Buzz, buzz, buzz!

"Go away, bees,"
said Little Chimp.
"Get away from me."

He got down
from Mother Chimp's back.

Little Chimp ran to hide
in the grass.

Big Chimp got some honey
out of the tree.

He let all the chimps
have some honey.

Little Chimp

looked at all the chimps

eating honey.

Buzz, buzz, buzz,

went the bees.

Mother Chimp walked away
from the tree.

She had some honey
for Little Chimp.

The honey looked good to eat.

Little Chimp came out
of the grass
and ran to get the honey.